D1715017

WILD MEAT

Carolyn Beard Whitlow

WILD MEAT

Lost Roads   Number 30   Providence   1986

Grateful acknowledgment is made to the following publications in which
some of these poems first appeared: *The Ithaca Women's Anthology, The
Massachusetts Review, Northeast Journal, Obsidian, Steppingstones,
Thirteenth Moon.*

Library of Congress Cataloging in Publication Data

Whitlow, Carolyn Beard
    Wild meat.

    (Lost roads ; no. 30)
    1. Poetry. I. Title
PS 3573.H4983W5   1986   811'.54   86-20814
ISBN 0-918786-34-7

Published by Lost Roads Publishers
PO Box 5848
Providence, Rhode Island 02903
First Printing by McNaughton and Gunn
Typeset by The Writer's Center, Bethesda, MD
Cover photograph by Perry Ashley
Book design by Forrest Gander and C.D. Wright

This project is supported in part by a grant from the Rhode Island State
Council on the Arts, and The Rhode Island Foundation.

For my daughters,
Joy and Abby,
who raised me,
who will love me when I'm old...

CONTENTS

South of Tomorrow

What Did I Do To Be So Black And Blue...

SOUTH OF TOMORROW

Someone must pay
for each shower,
unless rain.

At Newport,
the mansions
stand at the ocean's edge,
blocking the way to the sea.

ZUID BONAM 17

*Travel due south by North Star
to where a yellow road splits
the ocean in two
stars overhead.*

for Derek Walcott

Limé dolls in seamless Spanish
and Italian shoes stroll the Schottegat—
smuggler of pirates from the hollow land
and conquistadores, harborers of slave
husbands of inland shoals, where slick boys
dive sleek for coins and in the boat
market float fish of Venezuelan orange,
gilded gigolos, aloe leaves, and sweet
oil of Shell slips through—
nibble patois, kisses pâté,
taste the roux of merengué lips.
Beaded glass Nordic eyes stare, long
for dotted Swiss snow patches
and percale winds, quaff Amstel bier,
coconut crab and scallions, here, where
every other thing imported—more better—
catholics cross and only spices marry,
no need for iron or market of straw.

From the rickety skiff, gangplank down,
I skim the quai, wade the pontoon
one bridge in the Punda midst island boys
and misshapen Jewish ladies disheveled
in frocks who, to avoid the Inquisition,
flock to Mikve Israel, wail at Beth Haim,
lumber over andesite, Arawak terra
cotta, scale parched riverbeds, vexed,
milk the blood of saguaro, seek the healing
properties of distilled waters
bound from Coney Island
Square Garden, annoint hides tanned

by sun in waters of thirst with oils
of cod roe and livers, hungrily devour
she goat, draught from casques the sea
clarity of port, breathe deep blue
grass as grapes grown near eucalyptus groves,
and under a canopy of caliope green, hide
from dawn rain, rousing noisy nightbirds
in this land of the giants.

                         No anaconda
serpent here, or diamondbacks. Salt mountain
distances breach currents of sand,
shed their skins like snakes, rockslide,
avalanche to where pebbles spill
off the coast of the horizon. Marooned under hour-
glass, swollen rocks pepper the ocean duodenum,
surface layers, bottom feeders, breeders
of smegma and sweat, flounder, scour
the undergulf, peacock and parrot
fish, zebra and tigre stripes, mosaic,
flicker and flit. Shored with pungent,
wrinkled, lapping sounds, gauzy
shop merchants, caught between Wedgwood
and Stonehenge, softsell crabs, porcelain
by Royal Dalton and Danish wood, wind cut
on the bias, lace, perfumes, gold, papaya
juice, remnant batiks, alabaster, for gourdes,
florins, guilders, copper penance, sand dollars.
Here among these shallows, in the prattle
of receding shoal, I search for my name
and a man.

                         Jump tour.
By moon nightlight, tee-shirt jump-up, hip
fires tongue sabot snapped tambu, tuumba
drums timbale the streets. With the twinkle
of mountain house starlight the breeze
sifted pilot light in the starboard landhuis

window sights at horizon by height of eye,
shooting a star, six at the water line,
mustard roofs, the flaxen straw grueled
grist of maize atop blazoned white
unochhuis plantations of sugar, salt.
The Magistrate say paint all unochhuis
overnight or hang. Stark white
hurt his eyes. Pink, yellow gold, blue coral
flowers carnival the morning glory, agate, holy
mother of pearl, acolyte brass and bone.

While again in the grey silt of morning
raindrops drink petalsilk, I dream
that I dream. Wooden animals peck
downside the door, two parrots squawk.
There are no seasons.

                    In the blind
of mind's eye, as I lie in the brace
of your arms, seek truth, your mouth closes
like an eyelid on the pupil of my breast.
You rub leaves of three trees
on my honeybee wound, speak to me
in four languages. "Duchi! Duchi!"
My tongue is dry, sun glances the roof
of my mouth, quicksand
in the hollow 'tween my thighs.
I kiss your wetness,
bottom lip sea, top sky,
sail from star to star.
From the windmill well sweet water
wheels and swells over the lea.
Parched, sweat pocked, I rise
to bathe in the river
fed from the sky.

I rise and bathe, quicksilver, armor
for a flight south of the sea.
As the plane lifts over ancient leaves,
drifts beyond ice-capped clouds,
I feel like dancing barefoot
in the eerie light of snow,
crest an ocean of sweet light
and with siren grace descend
between channel buoys
midst a dipper of angelfish,
drink of their body and blood
for it is meet and right so to do.

A nipple breaks the water.
One circling swallow plucks the plum.

Somebody's calling my name.

TRINIDADIAN DAWN

Riding ever south toward Piarco,
Engine oiled, breathing tuned, regulated,

Cross plantains savannah-greened, palm fronds
Wave. Laughing, licking rotied fingers, lapping
Breasts of coconut pitched, laked, on night currents

Swept out by the penetrating stare of headlights,
We climb, soar. Rude grunting sparks irregular,
Groaning; grinding pinions, clutched, explode
The fullness of night, scurrying wild meat

Mangoed in matted undergrowth, startling
Overbush caned next to the road. Chirping frogs
Retreat cicadic mourn. Night stillness,

Tired, yawns,
As day breaks blue, drifts on Chaguaramas—

AFTER A POET, IN NEW YORK

I

I count by fives the days on the red bead abacus
Bamboo spoked, brass hinged, dark framed upon my lap.

Hibiscus sweet sun tea cools porcelained
In dragon cups Mexican brown, honey thick, china still.

II

Outside on the porch pigeon coo, the pebbled rustle
Of moor birds caged in acacia woods. Cormorants, wind

Torn, skitter and keel; a lone pelican adrift dips,
Blue tongued willow wasp hum. Carmine bee eaters

Prick winter thorn. Beneath the greened death dance
Of a dazed fly, slimed sea slugs ooze

The slick dredged sludge of swamp mud.
With salmon eyes I lick a popsicle dawn.

III

My wild rice paper skin trussed in eiderdown
Folds of flying geese, bent and untoward, feet
Inextricably bound, I stumble cobblestones,

At the weir spear carp lured with lumps
Of humpback bread, anemones; snappers quiver,

Charmed by tinkling, the jangled trill
Of silvered jewel snakes pit, untangled, wristwound.

Fish scales titter brazilwood cries,
Tumble as leaves slit from silt trees.

IV

I rummage in rising damp
For old herbs, dry rot, woodworm,

Catch in my throat the rattle, return,
Offer in kind the food you refuse—

Dried mallard mandarin, wintermelon
Soup, mulberry tripe, eggs swissed with ham,

Cherries fluted in pitted bowls,
Redseed, creamed mullet, lemon

Water rosé, cakes glacé, quince, nectarine wine,
The butterfly impress of silkspun hands—

V

I am the rock
You pitch against the tide.

My own voice silenced, my hands
Speak with your voice to the blind:

Last night I made love
To a man from Sudan

With your eyes—

THE VIRGIN MAN SLEEPS WITH A WOMAN

Old enough, yet, to drink, your smoke
Rings my fingers, neck. Your phoned
Invitation said match dressed
In black, daffodilled I sit. On
The platter carvings of ram
And fish, a pottage of ritual
Combat, textures of hair. Timidly,
You nibble an ear of corn,
Pudge the butter with bread,
Drumming mouthfuls of silence
In iambic sometameter with toweled
Fingertips and limpid tongue. We speak
Gingerly of your brother's race
To be grown, your sister's intellect
And petulance, your father's secret
Graciousness, his yearn for Yaddo
Where jangled fingers flybuzz
A panache of novel
Words and toe-tap phrasings,
A half-time show.
                              You say
You love to dance, even alone,
And in my waxy discs see Fred Astaire
Pirouette as I chant an organ prelude,
Whistle a snappy tune. Blue stockinged,
The waitress half fills my glass
Of tepid water, gives crumbs
The brush-off and clears, with grace,
Any mention of your mother. Over Port
Du Salut and Blue Mountain, we crane
Toward morning, lifting our cups in toast.
The circled flame dies like movie cowboys:
Without spilling its guts. Smoke
And sun rise. You rear in your ladder-
Backed chair, smile, playful, the way guys
Court Madam Alexander dolls, nothing

About you hard. Beyond the threshold
Of my porch I close the door gently,
Tight. Latch the horizon between us.
I hear the hum of your father's motor
Long after you're gone.

DADDY

I

Seminole. Seneca.
Iroquois. Burns.

Six blocks past
the Dawn Theatre.

Nine from Cunningham's.

By greened hedges
and dark oakened doors,

me and Daddy walked
hand in black hand

for a bottom shelved book
stamped in back with black star.

II

Our house was so cozy
Daddy named the resident
mouse Josephus. When Joe appeared
I was unafraid, his face familiar
as the lear on a turtle's snout,
the grin of gold fish beaks, Count
Caesar Dracula Beezago's bark—

We called Daddy 'Poppa Dude
Guy Man Pal,' giggled in awe
of his animal stories—how as a boy
he raised chickens for frying, pigeons
for squab, dreamed pheasant under glass
—how he'd heard, *if you cut the tail
off a dog and bury it under the house
he'll never leave*, how he backed a dog
to a log, then crawled way back back
in the dark beneath the Georgian porch...

At Thanksgiving we had a turkey
pick and Manischewitz wine, pomegranates
in summer and sugar cane sweet as
when Mama called his real name, Jim,
it melted, confectionate, in her mouth—

III
Daddy patiently married me daily
—him the preacher and the groom—
Mama sometimes the dried flower girl
whose scowl parched squalls, whose West
Indian smile blossomed rain forests
in Daddy's blood black Cherokeed eyes;
I did not know they loved til Mama

died, the only childhood nighttime
sound elaborate washing as they
each groomed for bed, scrubbed
tub hunched on cat paws, sponge crouched
greedy eyed, darting flicks of coral
blue fish afloat in the wallpaper sea—

On fishing trips by lantern light,
our riverbound raft unmoored,
I Hucked to his Jim, trolling
for catfish and bullheads, lioness
lambed, sniggling, him baiting my hook,
saying, *if you improve over me*
much as I over my father...

IV
I live now among the rushes.
Pinnacled above the ocean
under quilted midnight stars,
I drift asleep amid covers
and colors of unread books—
dream of the womb of my father...

A TEN-YEAR-OLD RIDES TO DAY CAMP

Pollard laughed
when Melba lurched
as the bus bumped over
a pothole/manhole.

He said,
"Looka that girl,"
pointing directly
at her. Eight others
turned to stare,
unaware that
daydreaming about
Pollard left her unbalanced.

She'd loved him until then.
Now she just held on.

MY BROTHER WENT TO HARVARD
AND DADDY BOUGHT A GUN

July 9

Senter denied he used his rifle
for anything but target practice...

Beard said he left with his daughter lying
on the car floor...

A white family followed him up to the road
and offered to be his witnesses...

State Police Supt. Howard Seiler
said Trooper Bement would not
have been justified
in making an arrest at the scene...

Beard said he was fishing at Crystal Lake
with his wife, Ethel, and 14-year-old
daughter, Cynthia, when a white man told him,
"You ought to stay with your own people."

*State Police have arrested a Holly,
Michigan man accused of ordering
a Detroit Negro family to leave
the Holly Recreation Area
at rifle point on July 4. Edward
Senter, 29, was arrested by
Detective Sgt. Gerald Corey and
Detective Jasper Brouwers last night.*

Bail was set at $1500.

July 12

The morning mail brought an envelope.
Scrawled across the article inside
in ink-red elderly hand—

...he should be turn free. innocent man.
he was trying to do something right:
keep the niggers in their places.
I wish we had plendy such fellows like him.

The letter attached read:—

Jesus Christ is God. John 1-1-18
            Nothing but the truth
Be not Self-righteous Luke 18-1-14
            Intergration is Immoral

Why should other Nationality group
of white people be surrounded
with the ungodly niggers

  ALL YOU NEGROES GO BACK DOWN SOUTH

The niggers are like a bunch of pigs.
Why cause the niggers come
where they are not wanted—meaning
the schools and restaurants, also
business place operated by the whites

President John F. Kennedy of United
States was a tool and a stooge
for the profiteering wealthy money
hungry Christ killing Jews, also
a nigger lover and a nigger vote
seeker and a joker and a psycho

SOME PEOPLES BRAIN IS LIKE A DEVIL'S
WORK SHOP

John F. Kennedy and Pope John XXIII
are both in hell burning
in the unquenchable everlasting fire
for the ungodly and sinners

Almighty God is the surpriser
           Death is noticeable
The soul resembles you
           Death don't wait for no one
Think it over

                    Signed—
                    Jerome P. Cavanaugh
                    City Hall
                    Detroit, Mich.

Odd! The envelope said:—

                    Albert Dunmore
                    479 Ledyard

25

FOR MY RED-HAIRED ENGLISH TEACHER, NOW DEAD

Thesis.

I remember only the tongues
Of hair licking out,
The knife sharp forkéd tongue,

As you stood me before
The planter class demanding:
"Who wrote your essay?"—

Chiding, what picaninny child
Would know what makes
A house a home—

I was fifteen.
Kept house for my mother
Who never had a pretty house—

But sweeping the ashes
From her brow knew well
The muse of hearth and home:

Antithesis.

Descant: Chant: Lullaby

Hush, hush, say not a word—sweet baby sleeps,
Heart cradled in her hand, so soft, so slight,
While silently, awake, grave mother weeps,

As yonder through fields dark dark father creeps
Away, twelve miles to trudge before daylight.
Hush, hush, say not a word—sweet baby sleeps.

Tucked, bundled on dirt floor, her sister, piqued,
Frayed, worn, on burlap lies, threadbare respite,
While silently, awake, grave mother weeps

And weeps. In apron starched and blue dawn sweeps
The night; biscuit sun rises golden, light.
Hush, hush, say not a word—sweet baby sleeps.

Out past the wooded burl spring waters seep
Down faces furrowed, warped, with cotton blight,
While silently, awake, grave mother weeps.

Beneath the one shade tree bud daughter keeps
The suckers, thumbed, of sugar tits sucked white.
Hush! Hush! Say not a word! —Sweet baby sleeps,
While silently, awake, grave mother weeps.

Strophe: Field Holler

In bark cloth frock, with wood brown hands splintered
And split, she logs the hours sweeping dust,
Suckling the babes and Mar'ster, baking crusts
Of bread. Her branches hold a sweet songbird,
Aflutter, dainty, gay; so soft, demured,
In silken feathers, lacy, hooped and trussed;
Whose warbled timbre echoes, saps. August
The nest built in that tree, rosewood timbered.

Strophe: Work Song

At corner auction blocks on Brooklyn streets
Knot cords of women brown of trunk with torn
Suitcase or bag. Day work they seek to feed
The sprigs of that oak forest. Perfumed, petite
But stately vultures dive for peppercorns
To grind and mill by rivers choked with weeds.

Epode: Duet

The sharp edges of the flat cut her—
Arpeggios of silence fluted
The kitchen. Mismatched dishes soaked in
The crack-filled sink. An occasional

Radio deafened the quiet. Jazz
Riffs cushioned taut midsummer night skies.

Her mind a metronome, Mama could
Hear a wrong note before finger touched

Key. Her older girl played piano.
Flies strummed the air in cacophony.

Coda: Goat Song: Minor Chord Blues

Meat loaf on toast,
With pickles and ketchup,
Tucked between leaves
Of waxed paper—

Elegant as served
On last night's crystal dishes;
Napkin so folded—
Cookies—two kinds!...

Synthesis.

Wearing pelts of rain, I sally
From my saucer, pour
Over lines, meter thoughts,

Cadence chiseled syllables into place,
Conjure her apple-pan dowdy,
Ironing crushed linen, creased silks,

Carving cane, corn husks,
Flywhisks, nettles
Under blue shirred swatches of dawn...

Now nailed to her room, mirror
Broken, buried face down, earth
Shrouds the stench of bones.

My tongue scrubs caves, searches for salt—
Trills a dirge with amazing grace notes.

POEM FOR THE CHILDREN

take your first steps in a Walker,
   come on out of your Yarde.
     Cruse the Jordan river,
       ride the Redding railroad,

catch a Coltrane.
   soar on a Scott-Heron—
     I mean fly like a Byrd.
       stroll for Miles through a Woodson,

 talk to the trees;
   bring me a Bunche of flowers:
   pick me a Rosa in the Parks;
    bathe in a Tubman

so you can babble like a Brooks.
  know the ABC's through
    Malcolm X, letters like W.E.B.
    Seale me an envelope,

mail it with a Stampp.
  Marshall all your strength;
    strive to know the Truth.
      introduce yourself to Lincoln,

shake hands with Booker T.
  learn for every wrong
    there's a Wright,
      and I'll crown you like a King.

SOUTH COUNTY

In Memoriam—
for Robert Hayden

I

The summer wind at Newport gaily blew
on sun-weaved frocks of silken green and pink
dimpled cheeks rustling cheery greetings through
the happy beach bound crowd. A tall, ink-
berry black man drove the decorated
dray, bedecked with ribbons fancy; flowers
rainbow made. No smile unlatched his dated
face, weathered, rumpled, cold. For hours—
under osnaburg, heat sweated and pale—
unbleached by sun, unwashed by wave of kind-
ness, in negro shoes he dragged to fill the pail,
for watered horses canter home. A wind-
route road to Bristol they would take in night
cool air, his singing high, black bird in flight.

II

Air cool, blackbird high in flight. His singing
wefts triangular midst cotton tufted clouds
furrowing: buzzard in checke̓d cassimere
courses round fist bolls; now hums, low-bellied,
low, a whippoorwill—a whip! poor Will—
blues moan; salt licks red striped back bent down,
rocking over loom of history; gin grins
threaded spittle colored kersey cloth; spindled,
amputated stump stitched neat, needle rusted;
hay stacked, stud horse unbridled, fed. Three fifths
guzzled 'fore, armed with Colts, blue coated,
men march toward the sea; Northerners, rank,
defiled, milling about the South undaunted
by weather, nor foe, now dead, for the Union.

III

By weather, or foe, now dead. For the union
consummated financier on field hand,
factory worker, day laborer, gun
toting water bearer; shy soldier's last stand
in shoes, russet hard leather twisted, soles
thick as wooded soil; single-breasted broad
tail coat swallowed, shrouding crumpled should-
ers, gold coast high collar buckled, clanked. Awed,
noble George Jones of Savannah summers,
Victorian, in Newport's cottage industry, gay
chateau by the sea, marbled walk aglimmer
in thrush-nighted heat. Clipper, fair Gaspée,
awash, aburn, ninety-six stowed, all dead;
contraband smugglers' rummed beauties abed.

IV

Contraband smugglers rummed. Beauties abed:
welted cache, flushed, chained, keens, straining leeward,
gives way, eyes furled. Mates crowing "Auntie Bell-
um," "jiggaboo," "niggah wench," wrench, cudgel,
reed, fustian laughs heavy, jocular,
then plunge. Futtock loose. Massive masts sway. Mist;
stinged singe of salted spray: improvident
implantations. Vessel lists; frigate cries
portside, gunnery booming; molasses
stained whitewashed decks sucked hungrily under,
Narragansett at bay; summer winded;
shore marish; horizon numbed, mariney;
sweet cargo battened down in undertow,
unpolished brass footlockers jettisoned.

V

Footlockers jettisoned. Unpolished brass
buttoned weskits shuttle permutations; smoked
salmon and cigars backhanded; raucous, crass
renderings etched carefully, ears cocked
round; whiskey straight; stomachs bulbous; truffles,
delicately scented, spooned from silvered
trays; guffaws, backslaps; violins a trifle
brash; bandy-leggéd gentlemen overheard
drawing music room conclusions: wealth
in black gold abundant; sugar, rum run-
ners afloat; war imminent; cold spell; stealth
apparent; footlockers jettisoned; guns
jammed; Mose caught, foot slaughtered, gangrene; mated
Dilsey, Clytie, Suky, Nel's Jane, with Jed.

VI

Nel's Jane, with Jed, Clytie, Suky, Dilsey,
sold downriver; fields fallow; drought; weavils;
Two Forks' 'ninnies auctioned, bought at fair price;
bid high, anty up; roulette wheel treadled,
trundled, thimble ball tumbling flat ironed
hands; cotton gathered, wool sheared; hemp spinning
rope tales; free news stories fabricated:
Pharoah's army got drownded; Marse Lincum:
savior; green maize high: tobacco burn; swarmed
bird caws: famine, livestock dead; blue coats grayed;
grey coats shrunken, bugle called; grainy mill-
hands brood; munitions plants breed migration,
circuses of crocus tamed; bullion stored;
bouillon served, chicken consommé, water.

VII

Chicken consommé, bouillon served, water-
cress; tenderloin of Boeuf Wellington cut
legal tender; pepper mill ground; shaken
Quakers tactile, textile agitators;
anti-abolition societies
full; Southerners satiated with blood
curdled screams, whip, lash; Woonsocket waiter
breathless, Paw tuckered; home enterprised; trade
off, manufactured; factions set; probate
wills; settled Missouri; compromised shares
cropping millions; prosperity rampant;
greens rooted; Browns empowered; black, soiled
credenza, polished; cantata, crescendoed
gaily, blew the summer wind at Newport.

AIN'T NOBODY HOME

*Ain't no
body home eight
o'clock Friday night*

WHAT

*'less they got some
body or no
body*

DID

I

DO

TO

BE

SO

BLACK

AND

11% CHANCE

BLUE....

*There are
23 million
reasons
why
I'd
beg, steal
or borrow
your man
for
one night
or
a lifetime,
Sister-woman...*

ROCKIN' A MAN, STONE BLIND

Cake in the oven, clothes out on the line,
Night wind blowin' against sweet, yellow thighs,
Two-eyed woman rockin' a man stone blind.

Man smell of honey, dark like coffee grind;
Countin' on his fingers since last July.
Cake in the oven, clothes out on the line.

Mister Jacobs say he be colorblind,
But got to tighten belts and loosen ties.
Two-eyed woman rockin' a man stone blind.

Winter becoming angry, rent behind.
Strapping spring sun needed to make mud pies.
Cake in the oven, clothes out on the line.

Looked in the mirror, Bessie's face I find.
I be so down low, my man be so high.
Two-eyed woman rockin' a man stone blind.

Policemans found him; damn near lost my mind.
Can't afford no flowers; can't even cry.
Cake in the oven, clothes out on the line.
Two-eyed woman rockin' a man stone blind.

PRESSURE COOKER

The day after Eve married O.B. City
he was tense and she was hyper
so she cooked to calm down and he ate
though they couldn't afford it
Each day while O.B. worked Eve'd
polish the furniture/scrub down the floors
wipe up the light film of grease on the stove
from cookin' candied yams/pork'n beans
fried chicken/collard greens'n ham hocks
green beans'n salt pork/'tater pie'n
choc'late cake 'cause he was a good
man and she loved him

Ev'ry weekend Eve came from Adam's
Rib Joint with two short ends'n white
bread and they'd drink to wash it down
In the summer when she could get a ride
she'd shop at the open-air market 'cause
they loved a fresh fish-fry

O.B.'s Mama used to drop by occasional to
check on their welfare but lately she'd been
feelin' poorly—told Eve when she called,
"I got low blood, Sugar."

> "Now Big Mama, you
> ain't been sick aday in
> yo' life. Why'ont you
> jest sit down'n res'
> a spell. Y'a know walkin'
> is a lotta exercise..."

When O.B. came home they ate.

ON RESPONSIBILITY: TOO MUCH
TOO SOON, TOO LITTLE
TOO LATE

Out of ignorance
and irregularity
you were born

menses are such
messes to keep track of—
they have no rhythm

what my mother
told me I'll tell
you: nothing

TRINITY

Old white men drive slow on purpose—
they have somewhere to go...

LENT:

Others fumed but he had no need to drive
fast tho' the traffic zoomed whooshed swished past,
horns honking as if the noise would clear
the smoke-filled space inside/outside

Now old, in tiger-like pursuits spent he
his fruitful years in purposeful pleasures
now spent, his only sugar a stick
to lean upon, his tree gnarled and bent, soft
though ripe, a lifeless form curled
like a kitten, a shriveled rubber band
an unblown horn, no rod or staff to comfort
only words and what we'd call positive strokes

He creeped. Each inch of pavement knew it
had been crept upon   he skipped not a crack,
every leaf/stone turned, crushed under the weight
of his tortoised pace. Cautiously, he rolled
and rolled and rolled, oats once sown wildly
now thickened like the chaff-chafing insides
of his thighs...

As the house lights dimmed his plot
receded a balding forest primeval:
a hair canal belied his root transplant

He could read while he drove, Dostoyevsky,
Bellow, Kafka—no rocking jarred the print
a time-motion study of his movements
calculated no action wasted as eyes flicked
left to right in deliberate sing-song
patterns cross the bridges of his scores

as though a sleek steel subway tunneled
effortlessly underground, funneling
him where he wanted to go in one
quick spurt...

He could afford to wait   he had been
where he was going, he was going where
he had been: a retraced retreat, an advance
on the past   a pervasive odor
in his mind and nose beckoned...

The car moved blindly forward like rodents
and roaches running over bare floors
and bare bodies barely forty years before...

ADVENT:

She'd worn a flower bed   gardenias
and chrysanthemums crowded her dress
and bunched at the waist   quickly, he
removed it so she would not smother,
ripped the unsoiled garden from its bed
so he could touch her earth and feel
her sky   he wanted her to rain

She tiptoed through life, having mastered
subservience to a very high degree
her eyes spoke through sealed lips

She wanted to get inside   in tune
in touch with herself, but he always
entered without knocking, bluntly
but with an ease that stifled her fire
her space was flat like the plane
of her stomach around its miniscule crater
no hills
no valleys
no peaks

She commanded commands
she danced and danced and danced,
but do ballerinas sweat? her life:
a repetitious one act play
an unstarred cast entered and exited
a stage left bare

Sunday afternoons she spent alternately
listening to him and the radio,
each voice drowning the competitor's
for split-seconds of her attention
alternate Sundays, she wept...

EPIPHANY:

Recognizable by her runned over
high heel shoes, left foot skewed
left on a right-leaning stilt
bangs pressed hard against her forehead
nails cracked and soft, bleached cuticles and moons
dirt washed away by scrubbing scrubbing scrubbing
her slender frame slenderized by table scraps
and water divided amongst five hungry
mouths clamoring to be fed

Faiths crossed and uncrossed, her hands
folded in prayer each night though sleepless
and restless they remained
her knuckles ached
her bunions throbbed
her baby wailed

The war widowed child-bride paid for her sins
each day at work the beads around her neck
filled her chest   the bedazzling jeweled
skyline beckoned   innocent temptation
stared nakedly at his face   the devil
spoke and he stole from mother
what he would steal
from daughter when ripe:
Hail Mary, full of Grace

MERCEDES

Stench of dead sweat reeking from God
knows which hole; wallowed in sallow;
from behind she was a broad
hipped buxom beauty; soft obesity
cutting fruit into bite-sized pieces—
stretch marks on crotch and stomach,
she wore designer jeans
that were not designed for her;
slept double-dutch in a duplex—

Mandrill: comfortably ugly:
belly hung low over loose lipped thighs, she
was aware of the wholesale order: he
had a habit
of giving identical gifts simultaneously—
a clock, toaster, untraceable rings—
late night occasional calls; pimp
walked 'cause his feet hurt; well known
for his well knownness, he could jump
high as two sheets of paper; Zoot Suit, he
couldn't come if she called—

Through lips too thin to kiss
she asked fo' the fifth
time, "Where was you last..." He cut
her off, skipped yesterday like a rope.
"You gon' do it?" he said.

"I don' leap out there fo' to play
ball befo' I knows the score—
Ain't gon' be no quarter woman
to yo' halfa man"—
He sputtered, repercussing—

Extra baggage packed, she railed
against him; mad as Miz Scarlet
lef' out, smokin', the next train...

Zeb and 'Zekial stood gaping
One say, "Don' that beat all!"
Other: "Stay 'way from it, Man!
Mercedes bends yo' mind and straightens hair!"
"I could see it, she was a stallion."
"Mercy! Mercy! Mercy!" Zeke, he shake
his head and moan, then say,
"Hold on: problems compounded and gathered interest..."

No wolf whistles met her at the whistle stop;
she got off shy, town bustlin', draggin' bags;
"Red Ryder" in his red roadster, go by
the name'a Rope Robingson, short stopped
when he saw her behind
them bags. Voice buttery, he say,
"Say, Bitta Sweet, let Poppa help ya..."
She start to snap back, "Look, Mista One-
Time," but she liked'ta fell out
when she beholt them almond eyes set
in mocha frosting, whipped cream
hat on his head. Two brass-tipped bronze
shoes stepped from the car under lean
tanbark striped pants. "I want you
in my space," he crooned. She 'magined
his jewels and felt like a queen. He droned,
"Com'on, get in." Mercedes felt her heart
attacked. "I got somebody t'home make me
wanna rattle'lem pots'n pans," she lie,
thinkin', 'Come by 'n get it, Big Man,
chow is waitin' on de peas.' By the time
he'd winked and smiled, she'da done time
for him...

Mercedes fawned, purred and pawed;
he petted and stroked; she bucked, bolted, weaved;
he rode side saddle; full;
she jumped Rope; she noosed him; he had her
hog tied...

Now the only folks in town working
overtime the gun company—
double-time on the standard shift,
so's when Rope slipped out late, time
or two, Mercedes unraveled;
she knowed he was double-time'n each
time he stood grinnin' fo' he slammed
the do', stingy brim cocked
to the side, overcoat draped splendid
from slender shoulders—

Mercedes was scared'nuff to run
offa the page; tried bein' sweet—
said, like Ronnie Isley, *"Let me down easy,"*
but he let her down.

Then she got serious as a great big dog,
said, fo' the fifth
time, "That's the last time
you'll hurt me"; Rope laughed,
packed a pistol, and knew that she knew...

*Zeb grunted and smacked. "I knows what's
comin', Man; somebody tol' me
his shit was in manure. Whyn't he just cut
her loose?"*—

Rope stole dimes
from his Mama purse, and church;
but now he didn' cotton no nickels
and wadn't astin' fo' dimes; he
needed her to case a bank
fo' a job he was plannin'...

Mercedes was always wimperin',
else she yelled a banshee wail;
had supper waitin' fo' him, tho';
one night it was so good he

couldn't get up; never;
then she lassoed Rope; rode him; took
his jewels fo' a prize...

Zeb didn' say nuffin' fo' a long time;
stood there starin' at the car.
It was red. A red Mercedes roadster.
"How come they didn' send her up?"

"...He was a nigger, Man."

'Bout that time Mercedes
turnt the corner, copper colored
blond kid led by the hand...

I'M A NATURAL

She flipped it back casually
with a toss a glance of
nonchalance calculated to look
cool coquettish unconcerned

His gaze grazed her
gave her grace
she knowing
shook her mane back
with a hip twist
a smug tilt to the left
as though a silent breeze
disturbed her locks

"Ummm-mmmm, Mama,
sho'wud lika cherry
offa yo' tree,"
said he,
bending slightly at the waist,
brim shading his eyes,
giving a four-fingered stroke
to his beautiful black-bearded chin

"It's all in the hair,"
she said,
"I'm a natural."

some babies cry at birth
some begin bald

SUPERMARKET BLUES

Ain't no call at all, sweet woman
Fo' to carry on—
Jes' my name and jes' my habit
To be Long Gone...
"*Long Gone,* "Southern Road

for Sterling A. Brown

I give away my lovin' like a grocer give a sack.
Say, I give away my lovin' to anyone who ast—
Cause the one I wants to want me say he ain't comin' back.

Cause the one I wants to need me done put me on the shelf.
Say, the one I needs to need me done put me on the shelf.
Say he done foun' another, he done found somebody else.

Called me Honey Sugar Baby, said I was his Georgia peach.
Called me Sugar, Honey, Baby; called me his Sweet Georgia Peach—
Talkin' trash til I'd go crazy; Lawd that sinner man could preach.

Nickel'd an' dimed me, Baby, but I give it to you, free.
Four dimes, two nickels, Daddy, but I give it to you free.
Lonesomeness fo' you, Poppa, make a paperbag woman outa me.

Baggin' smokestack ham an' poultry, streak a lean'n streak a fat—
Baggin' yam an' henpeck'd poultry, streak a lean'n streak a fat.
Stackin' butter beans an' coffee, any stray ole dog fat cat.

Say I give away my lovin' like a grocer give a sack.
I parcels out my lovin' ev'ry Tom an' Dick wid jack—
Steamboat Locomotive stokin'; engine, Lawd, done jumped
    the track.

Cain't catch that train, train don' run no more.
Cain't hop that train, train don' run no more.
Railroad Man lay track to Baltimore—

Now I'm a firs' class stevedore,
A firs' class stevedore.

LITTLE GIRL BLUE

for Michael S. Harper

Nina: she moan:

Sit there and count your fingers
ripple black bass blue notes—
graveled silt-throated postlude,
prelude of song,
scratchin' that old back door
where the sun gon' shine some day—
tympanic, symphonic, mechanic of grace,
major of minor chords, fortissimo, arpeggio;
trembling, hum mumbling
trumbles cleft treble; jazz razzed—

Nina: she moan:

Sit there and count the raindrops
pummel stones rocked, boulder pebbling—
staccato riveter; silver bell voice
diamond keyed; contralto cello; southern
bread rising sweet black wind swirled
blues song: rags and old iron; gin;
tender Memphis blossom torn; silkworm
sharecropper so longs ol' Cotton-
eyed Joe; plain gold ring chain ganged,
gang banged...

Nina: she moan:

waiting, a lonesome queen, on the Two-
Nineteen; mood: Indigo; trouble: in mind;
say: I tol' Jesus I'ma lay my head...
say: *Somebody tell my baby Sistuh—*
say: on some lonesome railroad line...

Nina: she moan:
Nina: she moan:
Nina: she moan:

WOMANSONG

for Zora Neale Hurston

Like dust spotlighted or sunlit glistens
Invasive, hairless, inchoate, beveled viscid,
Whipped incandescent whorls incipient,
Churns dense in incessant curlicue pools—
Then clambers, miasmaed, jumbled laterally,

Bundled translucent, swarms luminous, frenzily
Bumbling fumbles iridescent, twirls, radiantly
Vertical, funneled slipshod in ascendance,
Jarred, eddies canescent, dips faceted, descends

Measurably hesitant, siphoned whole,
Spirals multifoliate, consumed multiply,
Groundpulled irrefutably insensate,

Vertiginous, limps, centrifugaled,
Numbed, thwarted, humbled, drizzles down—

I'm tired of settling...

EMERALD GREEN, AND GEMSTONE BLUES

The glow of opalescent moon in stone
Cold sky; the gleam of glassy diamond peaks
Against a coral sea; the smell of streaks
Of emerald grass on topazed shore has shown

The jaded nature of men's souls: To own
An amythest or pearl of cut oblique,
Oval or square from Capetown, Mozambique,
Or Ghana, Guinea, Sierra Leone;

To harvest amber women, too, with lips
Of ruby red; to mine their men, the gold;
To take from them their land; their hope, their rights—

To raise a flag of sapphire blue chip
Stock and bloodstone, ivory trim bold
In bas-relief on starlit, moonstone night:

Carolyn Beard Whitlow, a native of Detroit, walked away from her Adult Education dissertation at Cornell to write poetry. She was encouraged as a beginning writer—however rigorously he opposed her abandonment of the doctoral studies—by the distinguished writer and educator J. Saunders Redding. She then enrolled as an MA student at Brown where she won the Rose Low Rome Memorial Poetry Prize. She stayed on to earn a following as an ardent, incisive teacher of creative writing, poetry and fiction by Black women, and special studies on Ralph Ellison. Whitlow is likewise known to be an inspiring reader of her own work. Currently she is with Brown University's administration. She lives in Providence with her daughters Joy and Abby, her cats Nairobi and Kenya.

ALSO FROM LOST ROADS

Poetry

Ralph Adamo, SADNESS AT THE PRIVATE UNIVERSITY;
THE END OF THE WORLD
Irv Broughton, THE BLESSING OF THE FLEET
Justin Caldwell, THE SLEEPING PORCH
Mark Craver, THE PROBLEM OF GRACE
Quinton Duval, DINNER MUSIC
Honor Johnson, SMALL AS A RESURRECTION
Frances Mayes, HOURS
John McKernan, WALKING ALONG THE MISSOURI RIVER
John S. Morris, BEAN STREET
Stan Rice, BODY OF WORK
Frank Stanford, THE SINGING KNIVES; YOU;
THE BATTLEFIELD WHERE THE MOON SAYS
I LOVE YOU

In translation

René Char, NO SIEGE IS ABSOLUTE versions by Franz Wright
Philippe Soupault, I'M LYING translated by Paulette Schmidt

Fiction

Alison Bundy, A BAD BUSINESS
Mary Caponegro, TALES FROM THE NEXT VILLAGE
Steve Stern, ISAAC AND THE UNDERTAKER'S DAUGHTER

Art

Zuleyka Benitez, TROUBLE IN PARADISE

Travel

Barbara and Sandra Heller, NEW ORLEANS MY DARLING

Rhode Island
State Council
· on the Arts ·